I0291523

This book is dedicated to Mrs. Johnson.

Copyright © 2025 Jennifer Jones
All copyright laws and rights reserved.
Published in the U.S.A.
For more information, email info@ninjalifehacks.tv
Paperback ISBN: 978-1-63731-933-8
Hardcover ISBN: 978-1-63731-935-2
eBook ISBN: 978-1-63731-934-5

Find the Book Hospital lesson plans at ninjalifehacks.tv

They were dropped and drawn upon
with pages crumpled and tales half-told.
The books all sighed, "We've had enough!"
Their once bright stories were growing old.

One day, the books could take no more.
To the Book Hospital, they flew.
Their bindings were so sore.
The bookmark nurses knew just what to do.

"My cover's ripped!" a book declared.
"My spine is cracked, I've lost my way!"
The nurses nodded with a smile,
"We'll fix you up, you'll be okay."

They stitched, they taped, they glued with care.
Each book was tended, page by page.
A cozy nook for them to heal,
a little rest to turn back their age.

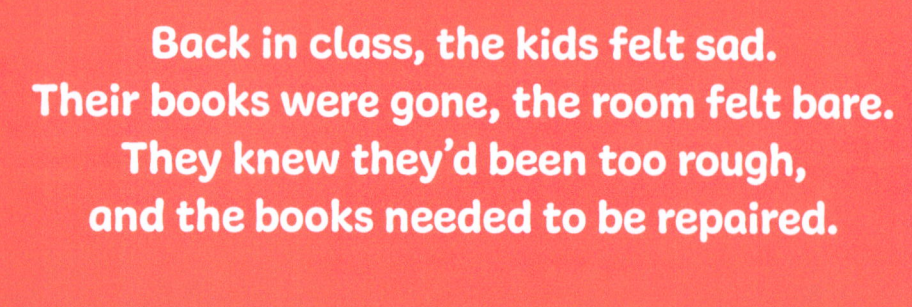

Back in class, the kids felt sad.
Their books were gone, the room felt bare.
They knew they'd been too rough,
and the books needed to be repaired.

So they all gathered, young and small,
to show the books they really cared.
They sent some flowers, vibrant and bright,
and shared kind stories, thoughtfully prepared.

"Dear Books," one child wrote with love.
"We're sorry for how we treated you.
We promise now to be better
and keep your pages like new."

Another child drew a sweet card
with drawings neat and colors bright.
"We've missed you, Books! Please come back.
We've been thinking of you every night."

The books at the hospital smiled wide.
Their spirits lifted by each note.
The flowers made their pages bloom
and brought them hope with every quote.

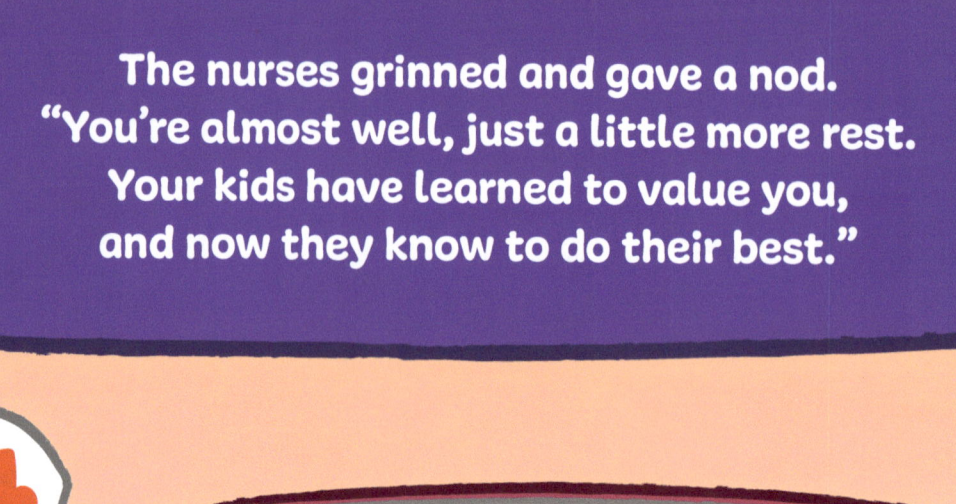

The nurses grinned and gave a nod.
"You're almost well, just a little more rest.
Your kids have learned to value you,
and now they know to do their best."

www.ingramcontent.com/pod-product-compliance
Lightning Source LLC
Chambersburg PA
CBHW041712160426
43209CB00018B/1808